TOMMY TRAVELER IN
THE WORLD OF BLACK HISTORY

Black Butterfly Children's Books

Text copyright © 1991 by Tom Feelings
Illustrations © 1991 by Tom Feelings
Production and design by Janice Walker
Coloring by Charles Eric Rodstrom
Lettering by George Roberts Jr.

Library of Congress Calaloging Card Number 90-071223
ISBN 0-86316-202-9

First Edition
Manufactured in Singapore

Published by Writers and Readers Publishing, Inc.
for Black Butterfly Children's Books

TABLE OF CONTENTS

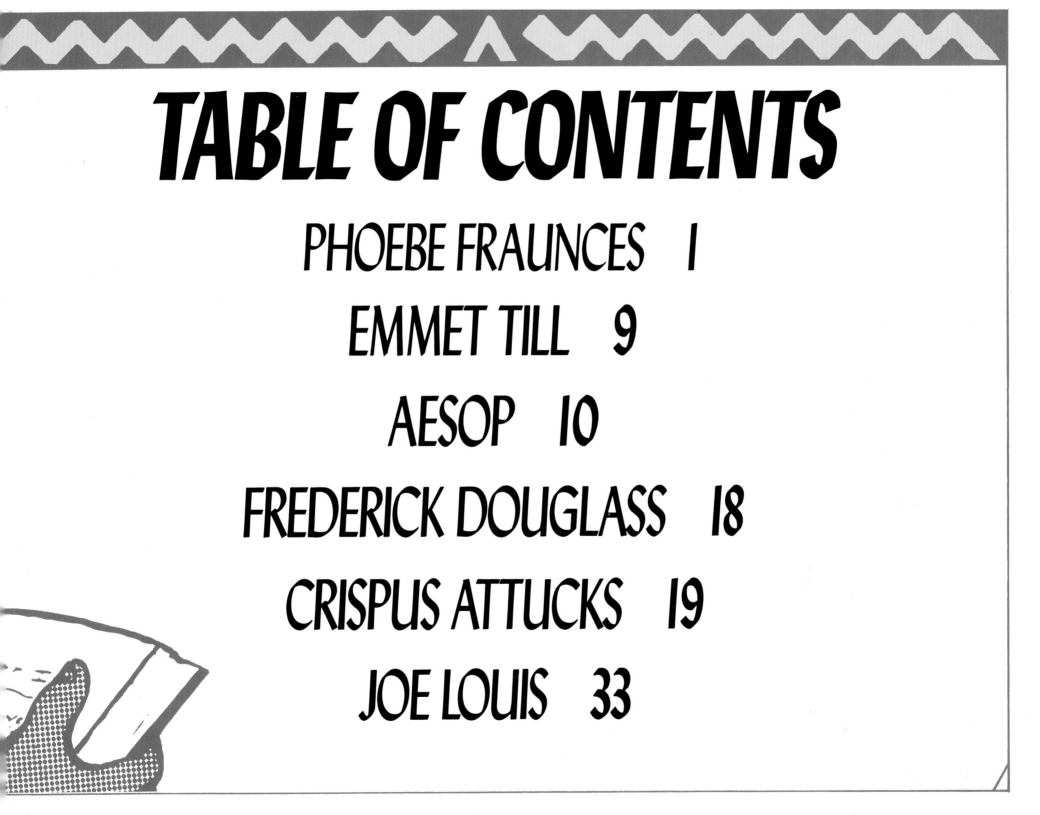

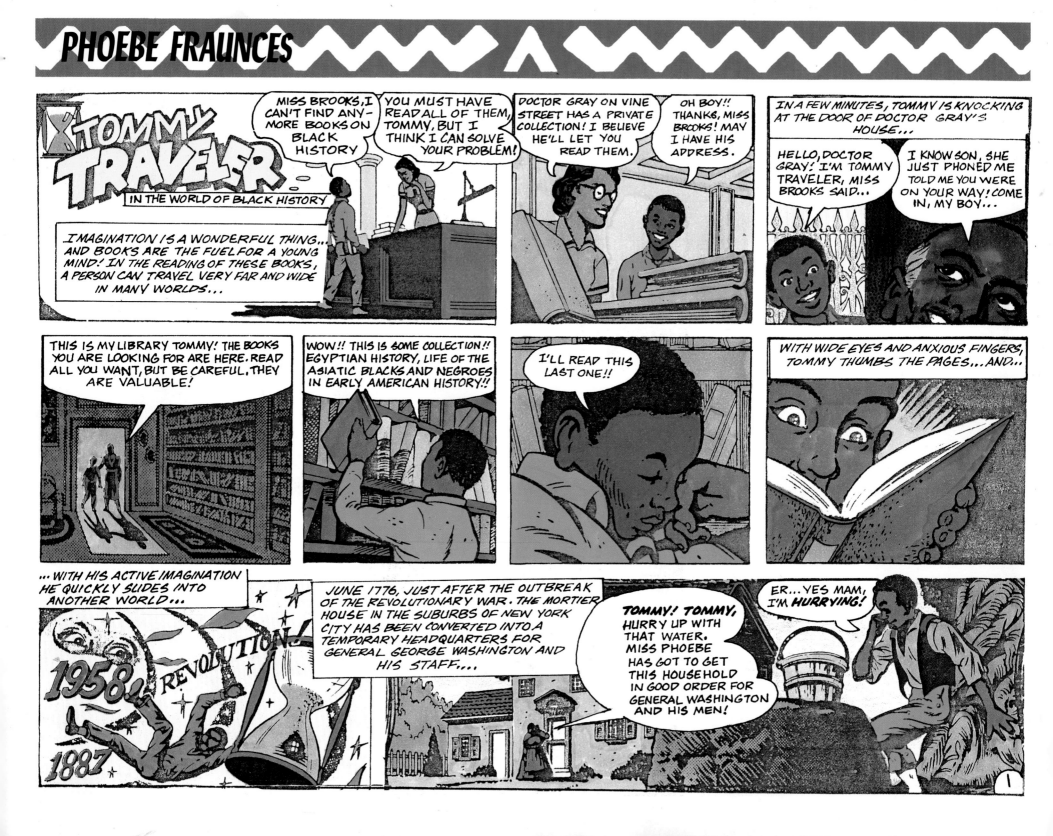

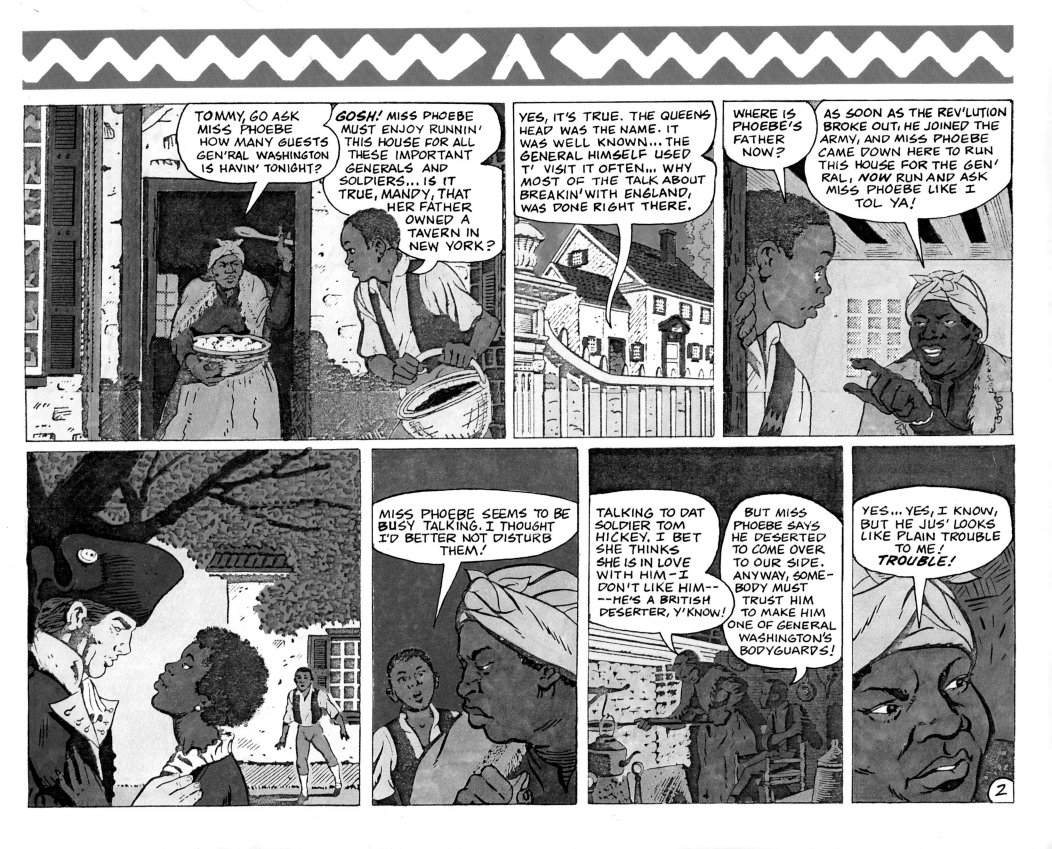

IT'S NIGHT AT MORTIER HOUSE. GENERAL WASHINGTON AND HIS STAFF—INCLUDING THOMAS HICKEY—ARE FINISHING DINNER.

TELL THE COOK SHE MADE A SPLENDID SUPPER TONIGHT, PHOEBE!

YES, INDEED!

VERY GOOD!

I WILL GENERAL!

NOW FOR SOME SWEETS. GENERAL PUTNAM, WILL YOU PASS THOSE LUSCIOUS PEARS OVER HERE!

HERE, GENERAL, I'LL DO IT... THIS ONE LOOKS FINE!

MISS PHOEBE, THAT PEAR!

OH, NO!

PHOEBE FRAUNCES IS TORN BETWEEN THE LOVE OF THE MAN SHE TRUSTED AND FOR THE LOVE OF THE COUNTRY, WHICH HER OWN FATHER IS FIGHTING...

7

STARING AT THE GENERAL AS HE IS ABOUT TO EAT THE POISONED PEAR, THOMAS HICKEY'S MIND IS TRANSFIXED TO ONE THOUGHT. SOON, VERY SOON GENERAL WASHINGTON WILL BE DEAD, AND MAYBE A NATION... HICKEY'S HEART BEGINS TO POUND...

NO, NO, GENERAL, DON'T EAT THAT. IT'S POISONED!!

POISONED?!

GLORY BE!

YES! EVIL MEN PLANNED THIS HORRIBLE THING. TOMMY AND I OVERHEARD THEM. THEY WERE SEEKING TO DO AWAY WITH YOU. THOMAS HICKEY IS ONE OF THEM!

LATER

THANK YOU, PHOEBE. I KNOW IT WAS NOT AN EASY THING TO DO. YOU HAVE SHOWN MUCH COURAGE HERE TONIGHT. THOMAS HICKEY HAS CONFESSED, AND WE WILL APPREHEND THE REST OF HIS CONSPIRATORS. YOU AND TOMMY HAVE DONE YOUR COUNTRY A GREAT SERVICE!

THOMAS HICKEY WAS HANGED IN 1776 AT GRAND AND CHRYTIES STs. IN THE PRESENCE OF TWENTY THOUSAND PEOPLE, SAVE ONE WHO STILL LOVED HIM... PHOEBE FRAUNCES...

PHOEBE FRAUNCES, WASHINGTON, HICKEY, 1776, PHOEBE WAR, PHOEBE PHOEBE

8

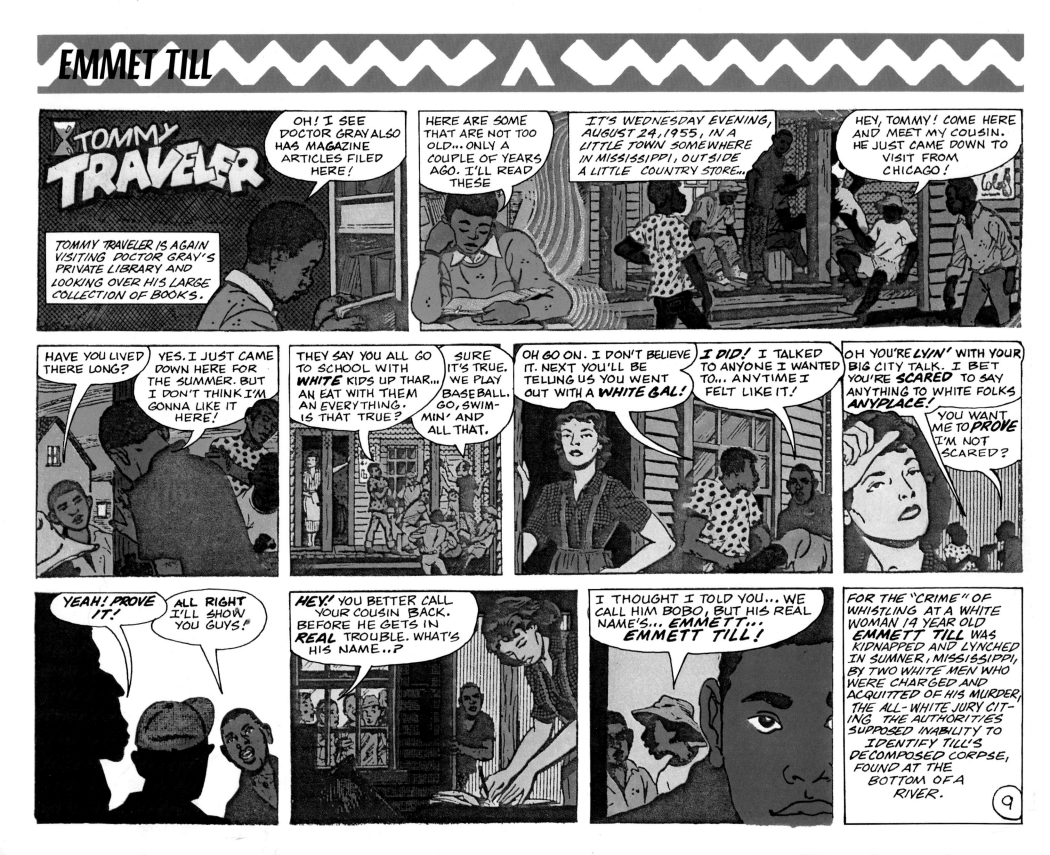

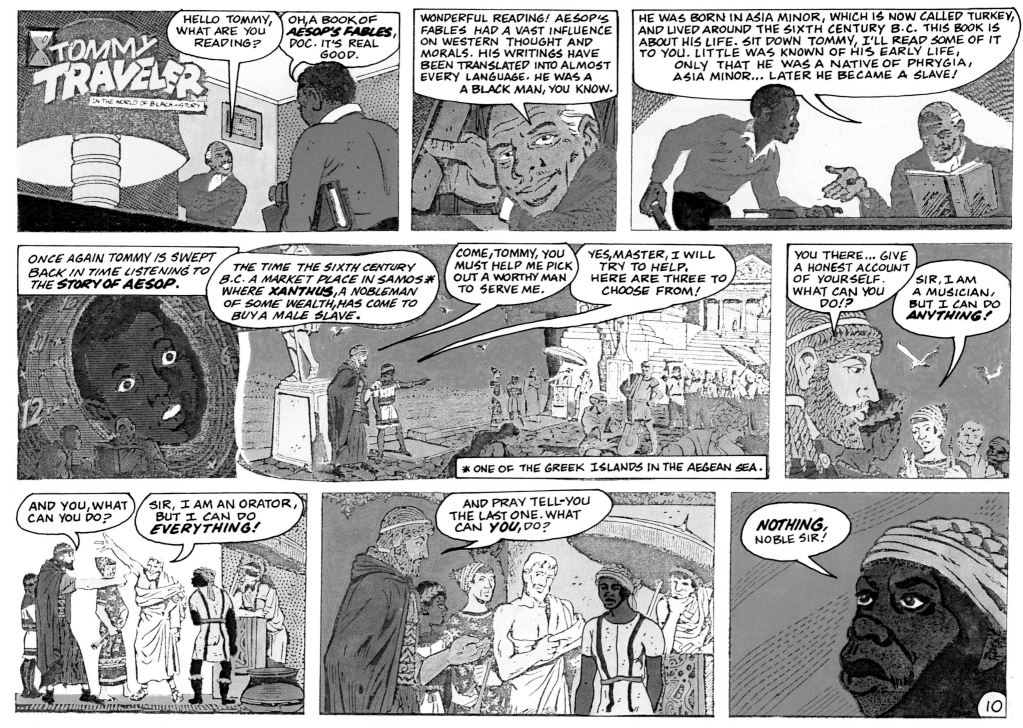

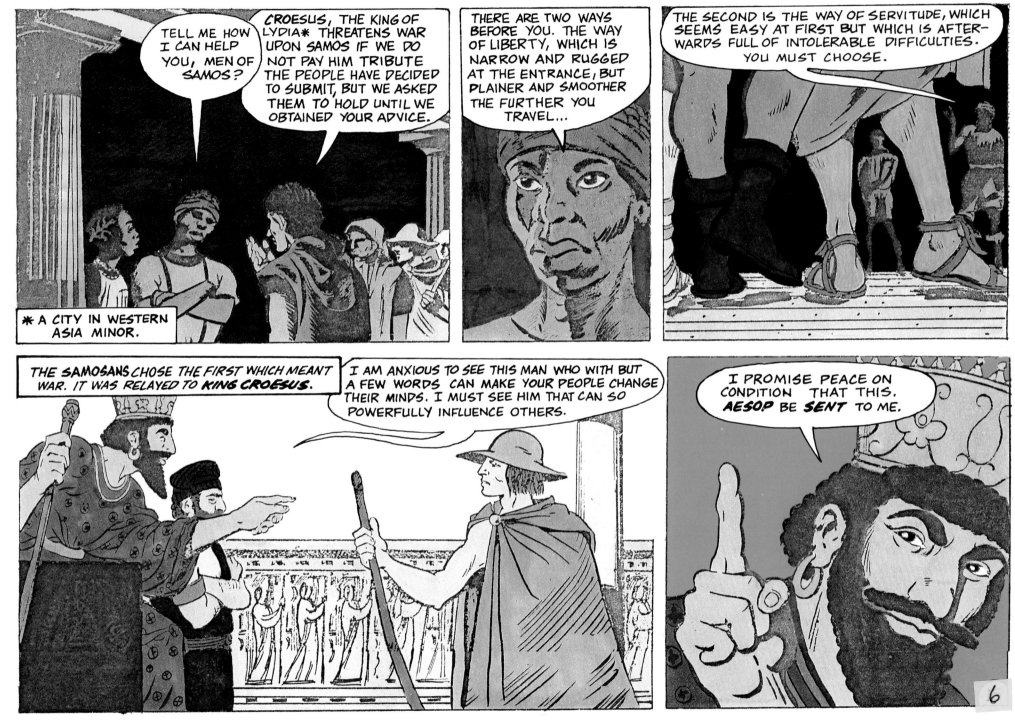

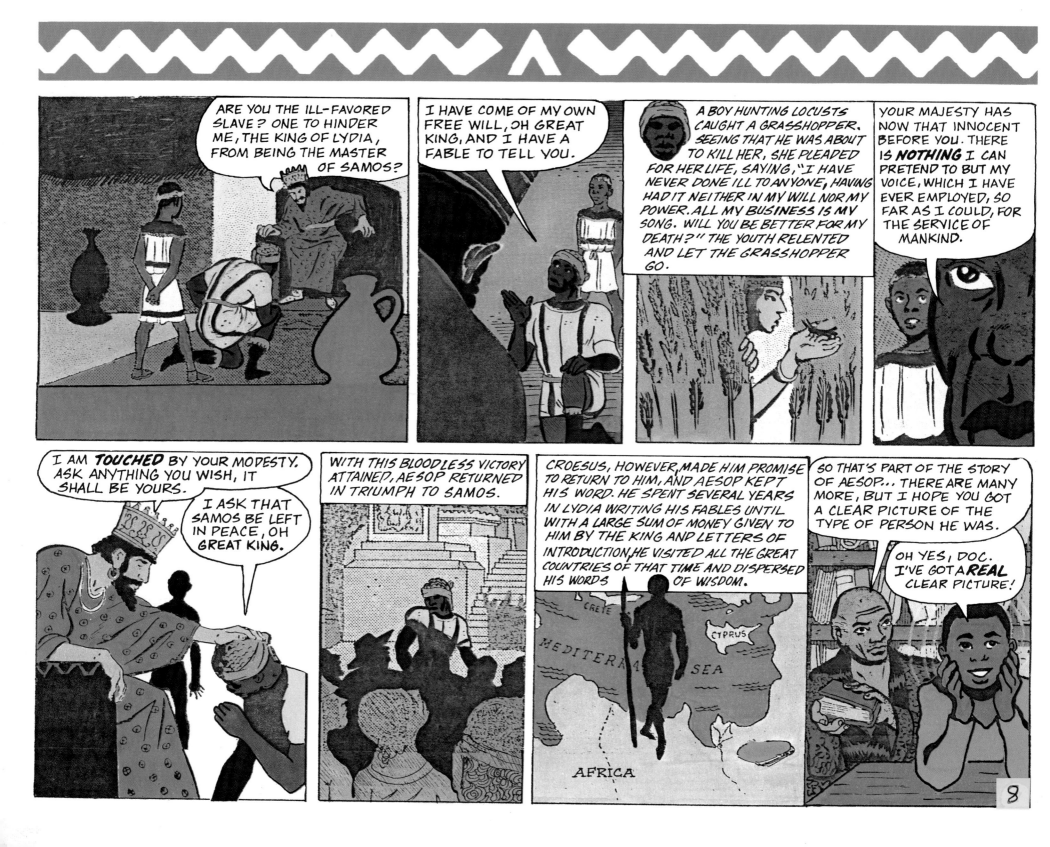

TOMMY TRAVELER IN THE WORLD OF BLACK HISTORY

I SEE, TOMMY YOU HAVE BEEN READING ABOUT THE INCREASE OF VIOLENCE AND LAWLESSNESS AGAINST BLACKS IN THE SOUTH.

DOC, IT LOOKS LIKE IT'S IN EVERY STATE? THE PAPERS ARE FILLED WITH STORIES. BUT I CAN'T SEE HOW OUR PEOPLE IN THE SOUTH CAN PUT UP WITH SO MUCH OF IT!

IT SEEMS SOMETIMES, TOMMY, THAT NOTHING CAN BE REALLY ACCOMPLISHED THROUGH PEACEFUL MEANS. I BELIEVE THAT SOMETIMES WE MUST LET IT BE KNOWN THAT WE INTEND TO **STAND UP** AND DEFEND OUR RIGHTS AS WELL AS **OURSELVES**, I'LL GIVE YOU AN EXAMPLE.

THERE WAS AN INCIDENT IN THE LIFE OF **FREDRIC DOUGLASS**, A GREAT MAN. I THINK THIS LITTLE STORY MIGHT HELP TO GIVE YOU A BETTER IDEA OF WHAT I MEAN.

...AS A YOUNG SLAVE FREDERICK HAD LEARNED TO READ A LITTLE. HE ACQUIRED A COPY OF THE BOOK, "THE COLUMBIAN ORATOR" AND DEVOURED THE SPEECHES OF PITT, FOX AND BURKE, WITH THEIR STIRRING WORDS ABOUT **LIBERTY** AND **FREEDOM**.

A PICTORIAL HISTORY of the NEGRO in AMERICA By Langston Hughes & Milton Meltzer Crown A.

IN HIS EARLY TEENS FRED TAUGHT AT A LITTLE COUNTRY SUNDAY SCHOOL, UNTIL WHITE MEN BROKE IT UP. A BLACK WHO COULD READ AND WRITE AS WELL AS TEACH WAS CONSIDERED AT THE TIME "TOO SMART FOR HIS OWN GOOD."

FRED WAS SENT FOR "TAMING" BY HIS MASTER TO **EDWARD** "COVEY, WHO WAS KNOWN FOR BEING A FIRST RATE HAND AT BREAKING "SMART NEGROES".

...DURING HIS FIRST SIX MONTHS THERE, FRED WAS WHIPPED DAILY, FOR THIS WAS **COVEY'S** WAY OF TAMING SLAVES

...THEN ONE DAY WHILE WORKING IN THE BROILING SUN, FREDERICK FAINTED...

GIT UP! YOU LIL' BLACK FAKER.

THAT NIGHT HE STRUGGLED. SEVEN MILES THROUGH THE DARK TO HIS MASTER'S HOUSE TO BEG TO BE REMOVED FROM COVEY'S CARE. BUT HE WAS ORDERED **BACK** AT ONCE.

IT WAS **THEN** THAT FRED, NOW SIXTEEN, TALL AND STRONG, DECIDED TO **DEFEND HIMSELF** IN THE FUTURE... THE NEXT DAY

COM'ON! HURRY IT UP, BOY!

FRED EASILY FLUNG COVEY TO THE GROUND!

EACH TIME **COVEY** APPROACHED HIM, FRED FLUNG THE WHITE MAN TO THE GROUND.

COVEY **GAVE UP**, CONTENTING HIMSELF FROM THEN ON WITH SIMPLY TRYING TO **WORK** FRED TO DEATH...

THUS IT WAS THAT FRED **LEARNED**.

WHEN A SLAVE CANNOT BE FLOGGED, HE IS MORE THAN **HALF FREE**. MEN ARE WHIPPED **OFTENEST** WHO ARE WHIPPED **EASIEST**.

THERE IS A **LOT** IN WHAT FREDRICK DOUGLASS HAD TO SAY... I'M SURE YOU AGREE!

18

TOMMY TRAVELER
IN THE WORLD OF BLACK HISTORY

TOMMY TRAVELER IS AGAIN VISITING DOCTOR GRAY'S PRIVATE LIBRARY AND LOOKING OVER HIS LARGE COLLECTION OF BOOKS.

OH! I SEE DOCTOR GRAY ALSO HAS MAGAZINE ARTICLES FILED HERE!

HERE IS ONE ABOUT A **CRISPUS ATTUCK'S**, A BLACKMAN WHO WAS THE FIRST MARTYR OF THE AMERICAN REVOLUTION

THE YEAR IS 1770... A BRITISH SHIP, THE ROMMEY, HEADED FOR THE HARBOR OF BOSTON, MASSACHUSETTS, CARRYING ON BOARD A PASSENGER WHO BECAME ONE OF THE LEADING FORCES IN THE EVENTS THAT LED TO THE **BOSTON MASSACRE.**

I'M COMING! I'M COMING, SIR!!

WHAT ARE YOU DOING RUNNING ALL OVER THIS SHIP? THERE'S WORK TO BE DONE.

I WAS WATCHING FOR LAND, WE'RE NEAR **BOSTON**, ARE'NT WE, SIR?

YOU TEND TO THEM SPUDS, AND LET THE CAPTAIN SIGHT LAND!

BUT WE'VE BEEN AT SEA ALMOST TWO MONTHS NOW. SHOULD'NT WE—

NEVER MIND, THIS IS A GOOD SHIP.

I CAN'T WAIT TO SEE BOSTON!

RIGHT NOW YOU SEE THAT THEM SPUDS ARE PEELED!

19

THE TOWNSEND ACTS HAD BEEN PASSED THE YEAR BEFORE, IN 1767. THE MERCHANTS OF MASSACHUSETTS DID NOT TAKE TO THIS NEW LAW. THERE WAS SOME TALK OF DOING SOMETHING ABOUT IT BUT NOTHING CAME OF IT!

BRITISH SOLDIERS BEGAN SEIZING MEN OF THE TOWN TO ACT AS SEAMEN ON THE ENGLISH SHIPS. THEY WERE *MADE* TO ENFORCE THE KING'S LAWS, LAWS THEY DIDN'T BELIEVE IN...

SOMETHING'S GOT TO BE DONE ABOUT THIS. SOMEONE HAS TO SHOW THESE PEOPLE HOW TO BREAK AWAY.

WHO WOULD WANT TO RISK HIS NECK AGAINST WELL ORGANIZED TROOPS? HE'D BE KILLED.

THAT'S WHEN CRISPUS ATTUCKS STEPPED FORWARD AND SPOKE!!
I'LL TAKE THE RISK. AND I KNOW OTHERS WHO'LL GO ALONG WITH ME.

WE NEED A MEETING TO FIND OUT HOW THE CITIZENS FEEL AND WHAT THEY WANT. COME WITH ME TO THE OLD SOUTH MEETING HOUSE -- AND BRING YOUR FRIENDS, THOSE WHO BELIEVE IN *FIGHTING* FOR FREEDOM.

AT THE SAME TIME, JUNE 10, 1768, JOHN HANCOCK'S SHIP, THE LIBERTY, WAS SEIZED FOR ALLEGEDLY VIOLATING THE TOWNSHEND ACTS AND ITS TRADE RESTRICTIONS.

22

CRISPUS ASKED THE PEOPLE OF BOSTON TO GO WITH HIM TO THE OLD SOUTH MEETING HOUSE.

THE PEOPLE FOLLOWED CRISPUS, THIS BIG MAN HERE WHO SEEMED TO COME OUT OF NO-WHERE, READY TO FIGHT FOR AMERICA AND HER INDEPENDENCE...

ONE OTHER LEADER WHO BELIEVED IN THE SAME WAY ATTUCKS DID WAS *JAMES OTIS*...

WORDS ARE A WASTE AT A TIME LIKE THIS. *ACTION* MUST BE TAKEN! THE STATE OF BOSTON IS THE SAME AS IF *WAR* HAD BEEN DECLARED!

OTIS IS RIGHT. STAND UP AND *FIGHT FOR YOUR RIGHTS!*

WE CAN ONLY DO SO MUCH. OTIS AND MY FRIEND CARR AND THE OTHERS ARE WILLING TO LEAD THE WAY TO INDEPENDENCE. BUT *YOU* MUST DO YOUR PART. YOU MUST FOLLOW AND *FIGHT!*

23

TOMMY TRAVELER

TOMMY IS AT DOCTOR GRAY'S HOUSE, LOOKING THROUGH AN OLD SCRAP-BOOK OF NEWSPAPER CLIPPINGS...

HEY LOOK DOC! A PICTURE OF *JOE LOUIS!* GEE, HE LOOKS YOUNG.

LET ME SEE, TOMMY.

YES, THIS IS JOE... TAKEN IN 1936, RIGHT AFTER HIS TWENTY-SEVENTH WIN, NOT LONG BEFORE HIS FIRST BOUT WITH THE GERMAN HEAVYWEIGHT *MAX SCHMELING,* HERE OPPOSITE JOE.

SCHMELING? OH, YES! I REMEMBER MY UNCLE BILL TALKING ABOUT THE SCHMELING-LOUIS BOUTS. HE SAYS HE WENT TO *BOTH* OF THEM

WHY YOU WERE'NT EVEN BORN WHEN THESE TWO FIGHTS TOOK PLACE, BUT LET ME TELL YOU ABOUT THIS FIRST BOUT. IN APRIL 1936, JOE LOUIS HAD WON *TWENTY-SEVEN* STRAIGHT VICTORIES. SO WHEN HE SIGNED TO FIGHT SCHMELING THAT JUNE, THE PAPERS WERE PICKING *JOE* TO WIN, DESPITE SCHMELING'S GREATER EXPERIENCE.

AT THAT TIME, TOMMY, JOE LOUIS WAS BY EXAMPLE DESTROYING THE MYTH OF WHITE SUPREMACY. AND MAX SCHMELING, THE GERMAN BOXER, WAS *MORE* THAN JUST AN OPPONENT, BECAUSE HE REPRESENTED *HITLER'S* GERMANY AND ALL IT STOOD FOR, THE ARYAN-SUPERIORITY THEORY AND THE DENIAL OF EQUAL RIGHTS TO DARKER PEOPLE AS WELL AS OTHER MINORITY GROUPS. YES, THIS COMING BATTLE HAD ATTRACTED *WORLD INTEREST...*

...THE NEWSPAPERS HAVE BUILT UP THE FIGHT SO MUCH THAT ON THAT NIGHT, JUNE 20, 1936, FORTY THOUSAND PEOPLE HAVE TURNED OUT TO SEE THE BATTLE AT THE YANKEE STADIUM...

LOUIS LOOKS IN MIGHTY GOOD SHAPE!

SO DOES SCHMELING!

HEY, UNCLE BILL IS JOE LOUIS COMING IN NOW!?

YEAH! I CAN SEE HIM NOW TOMMY. BOY *LOOK AT THIS CROWD,* IMAGINE HOW MANY MORE ARE LISTENING IN TONIGHT.

THE TALK IS THAT JOE'S GONNA WIN BY A *KNOCKOUT,* THEN HE'LL BE NEXT IN LINE FOR A SHOT AT THE *TITLE!*

ACROSS THE COUNTRY THOUSANDS OF RADIOS ARE TUNED IN AS THE REFEREE SPOKE TO THE TWO FIGHTERS

COM'ON, JOE, YOU CAN TAKE THIS ONE EASY

HOLD ON. Y'KNOW THAT SCHMELING IS A FORMER HEAVYWEIGHT CHAMP!

YEAH, BUT JOE IS THE LEADIN' CONTENDER FOR THE TITLE AINT HE?

FINALLY THE BELL RINGS...

CLANG

WELL, HERE'S WHAT WE CAME FOR TOMMY.

SLOWLY JOE APPROACHES THE COCKY GERMAN BOXER. NOT REALIZING THAT THIS FIGHT IS GOING TO BE THE MOST SURPRISING AND THE MOST TALKED ABOUT FIGHT OF HIS WHOLE CAREER.

TOMMY AND HIS UNCLE BILL, SETTLE DOWN TO WATCH THIS FIRST HISTORIC BOUT BETWEEN **JOE LOUIS** AND THE GERMAN BOXER **MAX SCHMELING.**

ROUND 1... RIGHT FROM THE OPENING ROUND, JOE FINDS SCHMELING'S STYLE HARD TO FIGURE, SO HE TRIES TO OUTREACH HIM WITH LEFT JABS...

IT LOOKS PRETTY SLOW, HUH, UNCLE BILL?

JOE CAN'T SEEM TO SCORE A CLEAN HIT. SCHMELING LOOKS LIKE HE'S WAITING FOR A CHANCE TO THROW THAT RIGHT.

LATE IN THE **SECOND,** MAX WAITS UNTIL JOE JABBED TWICE, THEN, SEEING HIS GUARD DROPPING, SCHMELING BRINGS A HARD OVERHAND RIGHT ACROSS.

HE HIT JOE SOLIDLY, AND IT SEEMS TO STING BADLY.

LOUIS SHAKES IT OFF AND IN THE **THIRD** ROUND, JOE CATCHES MAX UNDER THE EYE AND OPENS A CUT. BLOOD TRICKLES OUT BUT DOESN'T BOTHER MAX A BIT. HE KEEPS MOVING AND CIRCLING AND WAITING, WITH THAT RIGHT HAND ALWAYS COCKED AND ALWAYS DANGEROUS.

AT THE **END** OF THE THIRD, IN JOE'S CORNER HIS TRAINER BLACKBURN WARNS HIM—

YOU BETTER PROTECT YOURSELF FROM THAT **RIGHT,** CHAPPIE.

LOUIS MUST HAVE THOUGHT ABOUT WHAT BLACKBURN SAID BECAUSE IN THE MIDDLE OF THE **FOURTH** ROUND HE CHANGES HIS POSITION TO TRY ANOTHER WAY OF JABBING, **BUT....**

JOE REELS UNCERTAINLY AS SCHMELING CLOSES IN WITH **ANOTHER** RIGHT

TURNING IN A DAZE, LOUIS SINKS TO THE CANVAS.

34

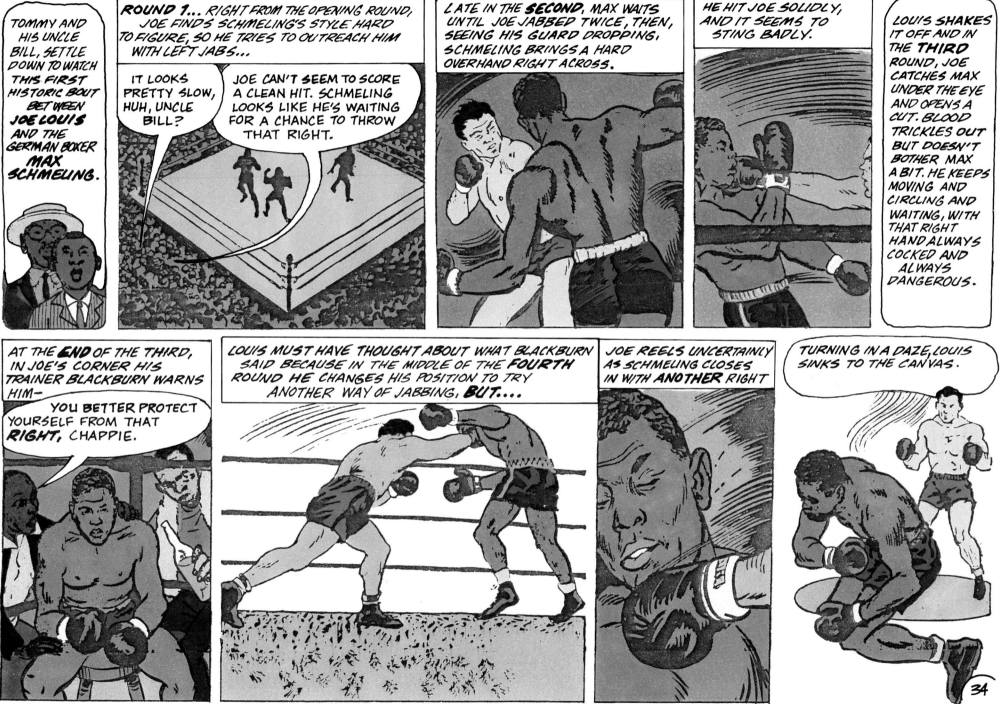

LATE IN THE FOURTH ROUND MAX SCHMELING LANDS TWO HARD RIGHT HANDS THAT DROP JOE LOUIS TO HIS KNEES—

AT THE COUNT OF THREE JOE CLIMBS TO HIS FEET... THEN

CLANG

OH, GOOD. THE BELL! GOSH, DO YOU THINK HE'LL BE ALRIGHT UNCLE BILL?

I DON'T KNOW, TOMMY, THOSE TWO BLOWS SEEMED TO HURT HIM.

WHEN HE GETS TO HIS CORNER, BLACKBURN WORKS ON LOUIS LIKE A BEAVER.

JOE, DID'NT I TELL YOU TO WATCH THAT RIGHT?

I TRIED TO, BUT I'M HAVING A HARD TIME TRYING TO REACH HIM WITH A PUNCH. HE JUST SLIPPED THAT RIGHT OVER MY GUARD.

WELL, GO BACK IN THERE AND KEEP YOUR GUARD UP HIGHER, KEEP JABBIN' AN' WHEN YOU SEE AN OPENING, CROSS WITH YOUR RIGHT!

ROUND 5... BEFORE JOE CAN GET STARTED, IN COMES THAT RIGHT AGAIN... JOE STEPS ASIDE ON THE NEXT ONE.

ROUND FIVE CONTINUES JOE KEEPING OUT OF SCHMELING'S WAY AS MUCH AS POSSIBLE, AND ON THE BELL ENDING THE FIFTH, LOUIS DROPS BOTH HANDS THE WAY FIGHTERS ALWAYS DO AT THE BELL...

CLANG

WITH HIS GUARD DOWN, HE WAS AN EASY TARGET.

35

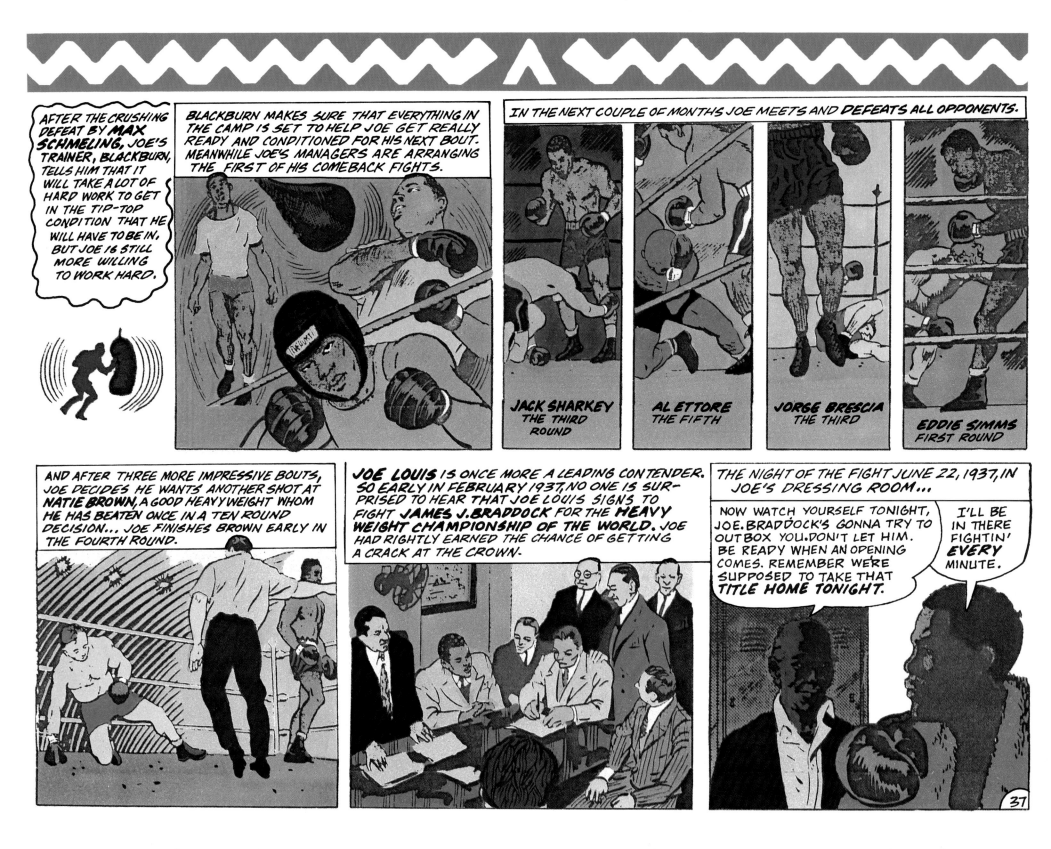

AFTER THE CRUSHING DEFEAT BY **MAX SCHMELING**, JOE'S TRAINER, BLACKBURN, TELLS HIM THAT IT WILL TAKE A LOT OF HARD WORK TO GET IN THE TIP-TOP CONDITION THAT HE WILL HAVE TO BE IN, BUT JOE IS STILL MORE WILLING TO WORK HARD.

BLACKBURN MAKES SURE THAT EVERYTHING IN THE CAMP IS SET TO HELP JOE GET REALLY READY AND CONDITIONED FOR HIS NEXT BOUT. MEANWHILE JOE'S MANAGERS ARE ARRANGING THE FIRST OF HIS COMEBACK FIGHTS.

IN THE NEXT COUPLE OF MONTHS JOE MEETS AND **DEFEATS** ALL OPPONENTS.

JACK SHARKEY THE THIRD ROUND

AL ETTORE THE FIFTH

JORGE BRESCIA THE THIRD

EDDIE SIMMS FIRST ROUND

AND AFTER THREE MORE IMPRESSIVE BOUTS, JOE DECIDES HE WANTS ANOTHER SHOT AT **NATIE BROWN**, A GOOD HEAVYWEIGHT WHOM HE HAS BEATEN ONCE IN A TEN ROUND DECISION... JOE FINISHES BROWN EARLY IN THE FOURTH ROUND.

JOE LOUIS IS ONCE MORE A LEADING CONTENDER. SO EARLY IN FEBRUARY 1937, NO ONE IS SURPRISED TO HEAR THAT JOE LOUIS SIGNS TO FIGHT **JAMES J. BRADDOCK** FOR THE **HEAVYWEIGHT CHAMPIONSHIP OF THE WORLD.** JOE HAD RIGHTLY EARNED THE CHANCE OF GETTING A CRACK AT THE CROWN.

THE NIGHT OF THE FIGHT JUNE 22, 1937, IN JOE'S DRESSING ROOM...

NOW WATCH YOURSELF TONIGHT, JOE. BRADDOCK'S GONNA TRY TO OUTBOX YOU. DON'T LET HIM. BE READY WHEN AN OPENING COMES. REMEMBER WE'RE SUPPOSED TO TAKE THAT **TITLE HOME TONIGHT.**

I'LL BE IN THERE FIGHTIN' **EVERY** MINUTE.

WE FIND TOMMY AND HIS UNCLE BILL AT HOME, LISTENING TO THE FIGHT.

WELL TOMMY, THIS IS THE ONE JOE WANTS.

ROUND 1, BRADDOCK PROBRABLY FIGURES THAT JOE IS A SUCKER FOR A RIGHT, FOR AFTER A FEW SECONDS IN COMES A HONEY OF ONE... BUT JOE STEPS ASIDE AND COUNTERS WITH A LEFT JAB.

THEN SUDDENLY BRADDOCK SLIPS IN A RIGHT CROSS THAT PUTS LOUIS DOWN... BUT HE JUMPS UP WITHOUT A COUNT, UNHURT.

BUT THE CHAMP THINKS JOE IS HURT BECAUSE EARLY IN THE SECOND HE LAUNCHES, AN ATTACK TOWARD JOE'S HEAD AND BODY. BUT LOUIS, SEEING AN OPENING LAUNCHES, HIS OWN ATTACK WHICH STARTED SLOWING BRADDOCK UP.

JOE TAKES THE LEAD IN THE THIRD AND LANDS GOOD RIGHT AND LEFT HANDS. AND FROM IN THE FOURTH ROUND TO THE SEVENTH, HE COUNTERS SHARPLY WITH RIGHT HAND PUNCHES. LOUIS CLEARLY IS WEARING DOWN THE CHAMP, BUT BRADDOCK IS A GAME FIGHTER.

WHEN THE EIGHTH ROUND COMES, BRADDOCK COMES OUT OF HIS CORNER ON WOBBLY LEGS. BUT STILL HE IS TRYING HARD TO HOLD ON TO HIS HARD-WON TITLE-THEN FOR JUST A MOMENT HE DROPS HIS GUARD, JOE SEES HIS CHANCE... AND...

THE REFEREE KNOWS IT IS THE END AND COUNTS HIM OUT.

FIFTEEN MILLION BLACKS, FARMERS, FACTORY WORKERS, CHAUFFEURS, COOKS, MAIDS, SCHOOL TEACHERS, LAWYERS, DOCTORS, AND JUST PLAIN KIDS-REJOICES. JOE LOUIS IS NOW HEAVYWEIGHT CHAMPION OF THE WORLD.

HORRAY! HE'S THE CHAMP, JOE LOUIS IS THE CHAMP OF THE WORLD!

YES, TOMMY. THAT'S RIGHT. BUT I GUESS, THAT JOE WON'T FEEL LIKE A REAL CHAMP UNTIL HE'S BEATEN MAX SCHMELING... AND MY GUESS IS THAT HE'LL BE GUNNIN' FOR MAX PRETTY SOON!

38

AFTER DEFEATING JAMES J. BRADDOCK FOR THE HEAVY-WEIGHT TITLE OF THE WORLD, JOE LOUIS TAKES ON AND WINS SEVERAL TUNE-UP FIGHTS AND IS NOW READY TO TAKE ON THE **ONLY** MAN WHO HAS BEATEN HIM, THE GERMAN BOXER **MAX SCHMELING**... ON MAY 19, 1938, JOE AND HIS MANAGER DROVE INTO NEW YORK WHERE JOE SIGNS UP TO MEET MAX SCHMELING IN A RETURN BATTLE.

JOE TRAINS AS NEVER BEFORE, AND WHEN THE TRAINING PERIOD ENDS...

WELL JOE, I GUESS YOU **KNOW** WHAT TO DO ABOUT SCHMELING'S RIGHT HAND NOW, I GUESS YOU TRAINED HARDER FOR THIS FIGHT THAN ANY BOUT *I* EVER DRILLED YOU FOR!

I'LL TRY TO MAKE IT COUNT, TOO.

JUNE 22, 1938, ON THE DAY OF THE BOUT THOUSANDS OF PEOPLE POUR INTO NEW YORK FOR THE FIGHT, AND THE ODDS ARE BEING QUOTED AT TWO TO ONE IN JOE'S FAVOR. BUT JOE ISN'T GOING TO BE OVER CONFIDENT *THIS* TIME.

BIG FIGHT TONIGHT

Thousands pour into New York for Louis

LOUIS 2-1 ODDS

Louis-Schmeling return match to...

DAILY NEWS

LOUIS FAVORED 2-1 ODDS TONIGHT

SCHMELING SAY "I'LL WIN AGAIN"

STAR RETURN BATTLE

DAILY SCHMELING-BOUT SELL-O...

THAT NIGHT IN JOE'S DRESSING ROOM, A FEW MINUTES BEFORE FIGHT TIME...

THIS IS *IT*, CHAPPIE. IT'S YOUR CHANCE TO PROVE YOU'RE A **REAL** CHAMP.

O.K, CHAPPIE, I'M READY AS A RADIO.

SEVENTY THOUSAND TURN OUT FOR THE FIGHT. THE REFEREE CALLS THE TWO FIGHTERS TO THE CENTER OF THE RING. JOE MUST BE THINKING OF THE LAST TIME HE FACED SCHMELING AND HOW HE WAS OUT-SMARTED AND OUT PUNCHED. JOE KEEPS LOOKING

THEN THE OPENING BELL SOUNDS, AND JOE LOUIS **CHARGES** ACROSS THE RING

CLANG

39

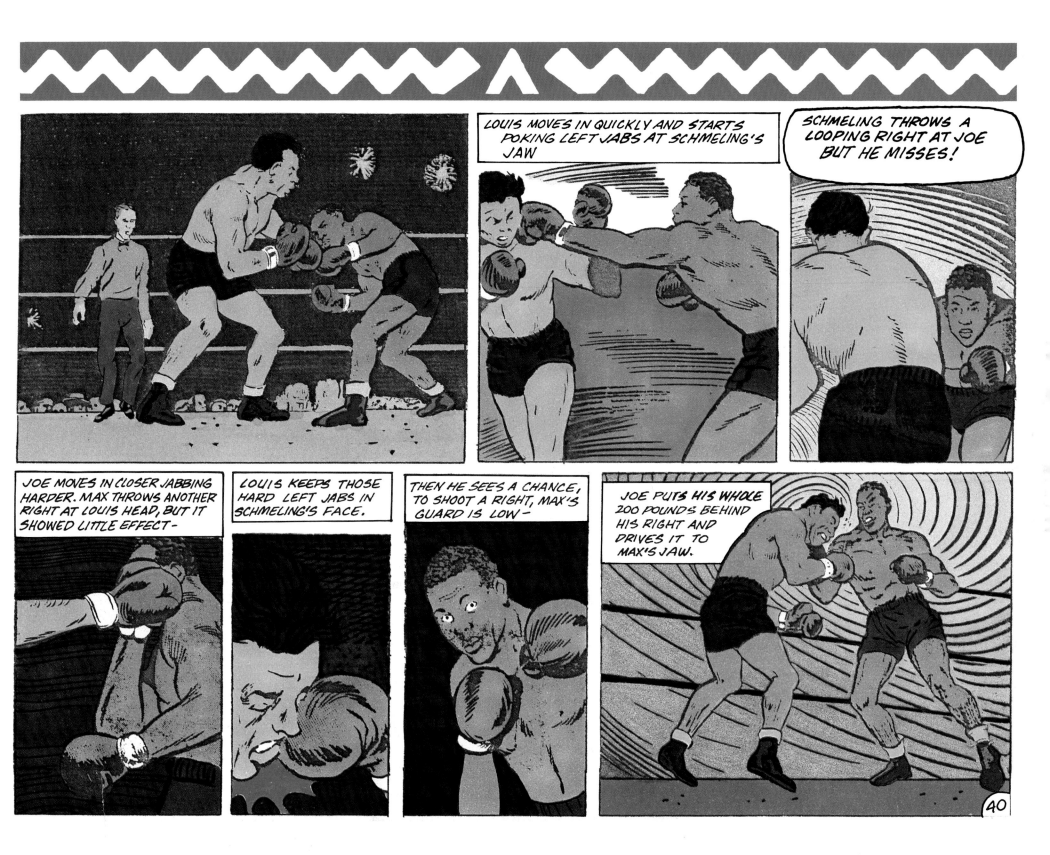

AFTER A BARRAGE BY JOE LOUIS, MAX SCHMELING DROPS AT THE COUNT OF THREE.

SEEING HIM UP AGAIN LOUIS MOVES IN FAST WITH A QUICK ONE-TWO TO THE HEAD, **DOWN** GOES MAX AGAIN.

AT THE COUNT OF TWO, MAX STRUGGLES TO HIS FEET. MOVING IN AGAIN JOE THROWS A LEFT HOOK, THEN A RIGHT TO THE JAW... **DOWN** HE GOES AGAIN.

AS THE GERMAN BOXER FALLS TO THE CANVAS, A TOWEL, RINGDOMS SYMBOL OF DEFEAT, COMES FLYING FROM HIS CORNER. REFEREE ARTHUR DONOVAN MOVES IN TO END THE SLAUGHTER. MAX SCHMELING **IS THROUGH!**

HE DID IT! UNCLE BILL, HE DID IT! HE BEAT MAX SCHMELING!

HE **SURE** DID, TOMMY! 2 MINUTES, 4 SECONDS OF THE **FIRST** ROUND!

THEY HAD LOTS OF CELEBRATIONS IN HARLEM AND ALL THE HARLEMS ALL OVER THE WORLD, THE NIGHT OF **JUNE 22, 1938**, AFTER THE FIGHT. HUNDREDS PARADED, DANCED, AND SANG IN THE STREETS. EVERYONE WAS PROUD OF JOE... WITHOUT KNOWING IT, JOE LOUIS HAD NOT ONLY BEATEN HIS ARCH OPPONENT, THE "SYMBOL OF GERMAN SUPREMACY," BUT HE ALSO SHOWED THE RACISTS OF THE WORLD THAT THE MYTH OF WHITE SUPREMACY WAS JUST THAT- A MYTH....

TO BE CONTINUED...

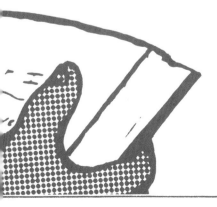

Tom Feelings: A Biographical Sketch

Illustrator, painter, sculptor, and writer, Tom Feelings was born May 19, 1933, in Brooklyn, New York. He attended the George Washington Vocational High School where his art talents were singled out, earning him a scholarship to attend the School of Visual Arts in New York City. During a tour of duty in the United States Air Force, Feelings worked in the Graphic Division of Third Air Force as a staff artist. Upon his return to the United States, he resumed training in painting and illustration at the School of Visual Arts. From 1958 to 1959, Feelings illustrated and wrote an original weekly comic strip series, "Tommy Traveler in the World of Negro History."

In 1961, Feelings traveled south to draw people in Black rural communities. Some of the drawings were included in *Look* magazine's comprehensive article "The Negro in the U.S." and *Reporter* magazine's landmark "Images of the South." The 1960s were a crucial period in the artist's career providing him with a diverse body of free-lance experience and national attention.

Tom Feelings has been a staff illustrator for numerous newspapers and magazines including *Milwaulkee Journal, African Review, Freedomways, Liberator, Negro Digest, Look, Harper's,* and *Pageant.*

During the mid-1960s Feelings served as an art consultant to Ghana Publishing House, illustrated the *African Review,* taught illustration, and exhibited widely in West Africa.

From 1966 through 1983 Tom Feelings illustrated nearly 24 books, many of them earning meritorious citation for outstanding illustrations. His published works in juvenile and young-adult books include: *Bola and the Oba's Drummer* (McGraw-Hill), *When The Stones Were Soft: East African Folktales* (Funk), *To Be A Slave* (Dial), *Song of the Empty Bottles* (Walck), *The Congo: River of Mystery, The Tuesday Elephant* (Crowell), *The Tales of Temba: Traditional African Stories, Sunaru: A Multimedia Guide For The Black Child, African Crafts, Black Folk Tales, A Quiet Place, Angolan Folktales, I Like Animals, Zamani Goes To Market, Moja Means One, Jambo Means Hello, Black Pilgrimage, Panther's Noon, Black Child, Something On My Mind, We Are One, Now Sheba Sings The Song, Daydreamers.*

Tom Feelings' works have brought him numerous awards and citations, including:

Caldecott Honor Book 1972
Citation — Brooklyn Arts Books for Children, Brooklyn Museum
American Library Association's Coretta Scott King Award -
   Black Pilgrimage, 1973; *Something On My Mind,* 1978
Woodward School Book Award, *Black Pilgrimage,* 1973
Caldecott Honor Book 1974
Boston Globe — Horn Book Award, 1974
School of Visual Arts — Outstanding Achievement Award, 1974
Bennial of Illustrations (Bratislava, Yugoslavia, 1976)
The American Book Awards Nomination, 1982
National Endowment for the Arts — Visual Arts Recipient, 1982

Among Feelings' diverse international experiences, one must include his tenure as consultant to the Ministry of Education, Guyana (South America), 1971-1973. During this period he trained Guyanese illustrators in textbook illustration. One of his former students is presently Director of Art for the Ministry of Education in Guyana. It was also during this period that Feelings began sculpting.

Tom Feelings has had many private and public exhibitions of his works in museums, galleries, libraries, and universities throughout the U.S.A., in Dakar, Senegal, and the Ghana Institute of Arts and Culture in Accra, Ghana (West Africa).

Currently, Feelings continues to work on children's book commissions as well as two major projects in progress: *The Talent We Possess,* an illustrated autobiography, and a monumental book on slavery, *The Middle Passage.* Feelings' works are currently being used by teachers in schools throughout the United States and appear in the following textbooks: *Flights of Color* (Ginn & Co.), *Dreams and Decisions* (Macmillan, Inc.). He is also the subject of a film suitable for classroom use. Presently he is employed as an Art Professor at the University of South Carolina.